Where Is Slug?

By Sascha Goddard

Bug was looking for her best pal, Slug.

Slug! Slug! Where are you?

Bug spots Moth.

She tugs Moth's wing.

"Moth! Did Slug come by?"
said Bug.

But Moth just shrugs.

"Slug! Have you dug
in the soft mud?" said Bug.

But Slug is **not**
in the soft mud.

Slug likes to get wet.

Bug will check the jug.

Bug sees a big man on a rug.

The man is looking at his mug.

The man puts Slug down
on the rug.

Bug and Slug hug!

CHECKING FOR MEANING

1. Whose wing does Bug tug? *(Literal)*

2. Where did Bug find Slug? *(Literal)*

3. Why does Moth shrug? *(Inferential)*

EXTENDING VOCABULARY

tugs	Look at the word *tugs*. What does it mean? What is the base of the word? What is another word that has a similar meaning to *tug*?
Moth's	Look at the word *Moth's*. What is the punctuation mark before the *s* called? Why is it there?
shrugs	Say the word *shrugs*. What sounds can you hear in this word? What sound does the *s* make on the end of the word? What other sound can *s* make?

MOVING BEYOND THE TEXT

1. How are slugs and bugs similar? How are they different?

2. What did you learn about where slugs like to live from the book?

3. What would you do if there was a slug on your mug?

4. What do you think Bug and Slug did after the story ended?

SPEED SOUNDS

| at | an | ap | et | og | ug |

| ell | ack | ash | ing |

PRACTICE WORDS

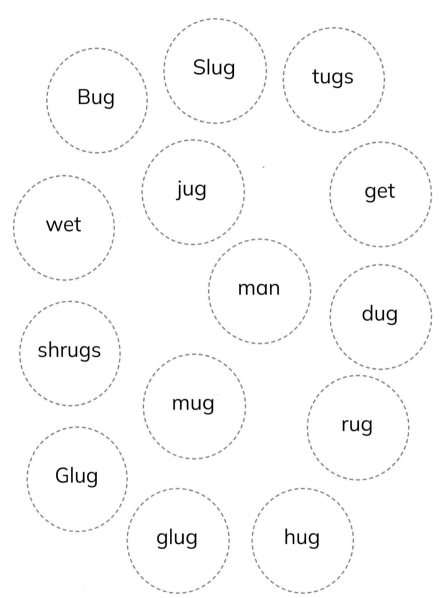

Bug

Slug

tugs

jug

get

wet

man

dug

shrugs

mug

rug

Glug

glug

hug